GREED

Wall Street Crimes

This book has been written for information purposes only. Every effort has been made to make this eBook as complete and accurate as possible. However, there may be mistakes in typography or content. Also, this book provides information only up to the publishing date. Therefore, this book should be used as a guide - not as the ultimate source.

The purpose of this book is to educate the readers. The author and the publisher do not warrant in any way that the information contained in this book is fully complete and shall not be responsible for any errors or omissions. The author and publisher shall have neither liability nor responsibility to any person or entity with respect to any loss or damage caused or alleged to be caused directly or indirectly by this book.

Table of Contents

A Culture of Toxic Greed

Wall Street is the hub of money since it encapsulates big businesses and bank culture. This money grants Wall Street a lot of influence over the economy and Capitol Hill. This wealth can be really toxic to healthy politics and free economy processes. This power and sway over the country make it really hard for the masses to get their needs fulfilled. This is because the political influence of banks through campaign contributions and lobbying can sway decisions to soothe their personal greed.

This is why it is common to see the skepticism and hatred that people have for Wall Street. Recent polls show that Democrats and Republicans both generally hate the rich folks sitting in Wall Street. On the Republican side, the bank bailout during the recessions was criticized for putting the American economy in serious debt, just to secure some banks. These banks basically exploited people's fears by stating that the economy would completely collapse if they weren't bailed out. Any other normal business would not have been bailed out by the government at the cost of trillions of dollars of debt; however, the banks were.

Many people agree that Wall Street hurts more than it helps them. This makes Wall Street a common punching bag during election season, even though politicians may end up passing bills that help them. Bernie Sanders opted for a line of attack using Wall Street against Hilary Clinton in the 2016 elections. His most effective line was to handover the transcripts from her speeches at Goldman Sachs. At the other end, Donald Trump also linked Hilary Clinton to Wall Street. As President, Trump ultimately <u>took fundraising</u> from Wall Street himself. This is the level of sway that Wall Street has on politics and the economy.

Banks used to work on the basis of risk management; they just had to make sure that they earned more than they lost. Traders began to invest in businesses and then double the worth of their shares by increasing public interest in that company. By the year 2000, Wall Street's culture primarily revolved around greed and toxicity. The role of deregulation on the banks caused traders to move toward publically owned investment banks. They moved onto companies that had financial filings with the SEC and stock listings in the

New York Stock Exchange. This formed megabanks like JP Morgan and Citigroup. They had hundreds of thousands of employees with ties all over the world. The bureaucratic powers they held ensured that they could divulge into diverse businesses, which meant they spanned over virtually the entire world. Investment banks actually turned into models of loose confederation units. The only thing that connected the vast army of employees was the source of cheap money through government subsidized debt and bank deposits.

Every manager working at these banks wanted a bigger slice of the pie. The easy money made these investment banks think that they were too big to fail. The sheer size didn't highlight that smaller assets of dubious quality meant that they would definitely fail. In 2007, the small rotten foundation assets completely collapsed, ensuring that the whole organization fell as well. This bought the crisis that almost finished Wall Street.

The greed of Wall Street led to its downfall once, but they may not have learned the lesson. Although the economy is largely back on track, they still continue to produce traders who think that they are above the law. However, it is definitely not true. There are many traders who gave in to their greed and began to meddle with the system to make their easy cash. This potentially caused the downfall of the economy a decade ago. It is important to note that even the most notorious of Wall Street white criminals were caught eventually.

Notorious Wall Street Traders

For a long time, the greed of Wall Street traders went unchecked. Their influence over the political and economic climate of the country made them think that they were above the law. However, money couldn't get them out of every crime that they committed. These traders tried to play the game, but their fraud and Ponzi schemes led to dire consequences. There are 15 notorious Wall Street criminals who were caught for stealing and money laundering. Their crimes led to a lot of harm to the economic situation of many people around the globe.

Michael Milken

Michael Robert Milken is an American financier who became famous when he was charged with 98 counts of fraud and racketeering in 1990. He was born in 1946 and received his MBA from the University of Pennsylvania. He was once the main bond trader in Former Drexel Burnham Lambert. He was the mind behind high-yield or junk bonds during the 1980s. His high-yield bond trading department led to a 100% return on investment, making him one of the most brilliant financial traders at the company.

He leveraged a buy-out for companies who were almost shut out of the market because of their low credit scores. This system of trading bonds is still in place because it was surely a great way to accumulate wealth and save jobs. By 1976, he was making an estimate of $5 million a year. However, soon the success started going to his head and being a millionaire wasn't enough.

He began to indulge in illegal transactions and used tactics like stock manipulation, insider trading, fraud, and even buying stocks on behalf of other people. He facilitated many activities of LBO firms like green mailers and Kohlberg Kravis Roberts. Milken leveraged great buyouts with a highly confidential letter from Drexel that promised to raise the debt in time to fulfill the obligations by the buyer. However, this letter wasn't actually true but was the perfect tool to create a market for any sort of bond. The letters demonstrated the ability of the client to pay the loan even if they did not actually have the financial prowess to do so.

He soon became the face of a large insider trading investigation and pleaded guilty to six counts of tax and securities violations in

1990. Milken even had to pay approximately $1.1 billion in fines to the SEC, court, and Drexel investors. He also faced a lifetime ban on involvement in the industry of securities and served 22 months in jail.

His crimes have been widely debated. Milken believed that the regulations and rules under securities law hindered the free flow of trade. Many argue that Milken never actually performed any illegal acts but encouraged his colleagues to do them on his behalf. Whatever the case, Milken did indeed use the law as more of a suggestion. His career as a trader led to him accumulating wealth really quickly and the rate at which his bank account filled shows that it wasn't entirely legal.

Barry Minkow

Barry Jay Minkow was born in 1966 and was a former American businessman. He founded the ZZZZ Best business while he was still in high school. On the surface, the company appeared to be a restoration and carpet-cleaning company. However, the business was actually a front to attract potential investors in a huge Ponzi scheme. In the beginning, Minkow actually stole his family's jewelry, staged break-ins, ran up fraud credit cards, and used check kiting to create for his 'company'.

He created a series of fake documents and even rented offices to appear like a legitimate company after he set up an insurance restoration business. The restoration business was called Interstate Appraisal Services. Banks began to invest in the company and all of this cash went straight into Minkow's pockets.

He invested some of this cash into ZZZZ Best and it was actually applauded for the quality of its services in many places. He raised money with floating funds with different banks and factoring his accounts receivable for work under contracts. One major mistake he made was taking the company public and investigators soon found that only 14% of revenue by ZZZZ Best was actually real. It collapsed in 1987 and ended up costing lenders and investors a huge amount of $100 million.

This was one of the biggest investment and accounting frauds ever performed by a single person. This Ponzi scheme actually became a model for many other ventures started by criminals all over the world. It is one of the largest investment frauds ever perpetrated by a single person, as well as one of the largest accounting frauds in history. The scheme is often used as a case study of accounting fraud.

In 1988, Minkow was charged with 54 counts of money laundering, mail fraud, securities fraud, embezzlement, bank fraud, and tax evasion. He was sentenced to 25 years in prison and released in 1995. He didn't learn much from his 25 years in jail because he was recently convicted for mail fraud and insider trading and put back into prison. He admitted to deliberately driving down the stock price of a homebuilder and five more years were added to his prison time. Three years later, while still in prison, another five years were added as he was convicted for defrauding his own Church. He has to now pay $612 million in restitution to various parties.

Jordan Belfort

Jordan Ross Belfort was born in 1962 and is an American author and former stockbroker. In 1999, he pled guilty to stock-market manipulation, fraud, and penny-stock scams. His memoir has been adapted to a film called The Wolf of Wall Street starring Leonardo DiCaprio. He dropped out of dental school early on when he found that he would not be able to make a lot of money with that career. He got a job as a stockbroker at L.F. Rothschild when he was 25 years old. He became enamored with the fast-paced lavish lifestyle of the rich and he founded a brokerage firm called Stratton Oakmont.

While at L.F. Rothschild, he merely learned the intricacies of the financial system but this firm was the main mechanism through which he committed a majority of his crimes. On the front, it was based as a 'boiler room' firm that marketed illiquid securities like penny stocks. However, investigators found that Belfort and his employees working at Stratton actually worked under 'pump and dump' schemes. These were designed to enrich old investors and defraud the new ones.

Pump and dump schemes are a form of securities fraud that involved artificially inflating the price of a stock. Belfort managed to do this by inflating the price through misleading positive statements which were simply false. The scores of profits he made were by buying cheap stock and selling it for a higher price to different investors. When the stocks became common and people began investing in them, this inflated the price of the stocks even more. After selling as much as they could, they pulled dumped the whole lot. When all the stocks were essentially 'dumped', the overvalued shares actually fell in price resulting in a major loss for the investors.

The company granted him enough money to lead a very lavish lifestyle and he indulged in the extensive use of recreational drugs. He was also an addiction to methaqualone, which he bought under the name of Quaalude. At one point, his company was so vast that he managed over 1,000 stockbrokers and issued stocks worth more than US$1 billion.

In 1998, his company was shut down and Belfort was indicted for money laundering and securities fraud. His investors lost over $200 million due to the investigation and company shut down. He cooperated with the FBI and gave testimonies against subordinates and partners in his fraudulent scheme. This granted him 22 months in prison and $110.4 million in fines and fees.

Bernard Madoff

Bernard Lawrence Madoff was born in 1938 and is a former investment advisor, marker market, and financier. He is currently in federal prison for his extensive crimes related to the huge Ponzi scheme he began which has been estimated at $64.8 billion.

He was appointed as the non-executive chairman of NASDAQ stock market where the biggest Ponzi scheme the world has ever seen was launched. He actually took money from over 4,800 clients till 2008 when he was arrested. He lived off the profits for years along with his brother, Peter. The scheme was launched when Bernard Madoff founded a penny stock brokerage firm in 1960. This small business turned into Bernard L. Madoff Investment Securities where he served as chairman until he was finally arrested in 2008.

The company expanded quickly as one of the top market maker businesses on Wall Street. It directly issued executive orders from retail brokers which bypassed 'specialist' firms over the counter. His brother, Peter Madoff, was hired as the senior managing director and Peter's daughter, Shana Madoff, was the chief compliance officer. Peter Madoff was also sentenced to 10 years in prison while Bernard Madoff sentenced to 150 years in jail. Peter's son committed suicide two years after his father's arrest.

Madoff would indulge in asset management which was later dubbed as the Jewish Bond. These many hedge funds were famous for making huge above average gains every year. His continued success every year was a little suspicious as even the best traders face losses some time or the other. Several investigations were launched into the company by the US Securities and Exchange Commission (SEC) but did not have a clue about the massive fraud taking place in the company.

In 2008, Madoff's own sons contacted the authorities after Madoff confessed to them that the asset management department of his firm was a Ponzi scheme. He confessed by saying that his company was 'all a big lie' when he had trouble with a large series of redemptions from investors. He was arrested the very next day with one count of security fraud. In 2009, Madoff pled guilty to 11 federal felonies and admitted guilt for launching the billion dollar investment scheme. Although he suggested that the Ponzi scheme began in the 1990s, investigators found that the fraud actually may have begun in 1970s. Including fabricated gains, the amounts missing from the investors and clientele bank accounts was almost $65 billion.

Raj Rajaratnam

Raj Rajaratnam was born in 1957 and was a Sri-Lankan-American hedge fund manager.

He founded the Galleon Group in New York. Currently, Rajaratnam is confined at a Federal Medical Center in Devens, Massachusetts. It is an administrative facility that provides mental and medical healthcare to male offenders. He will be released from this confinement in 2021. But why is he in prison?

He started his career as a loan officer in a company called Chase and focused on the technology sector. His first job as a tech stock analyst was for Needham & Co from where he learned the financial sector's ins and outs. He founded the Galleon Group based on his knowledge from there. The company eventually grew saw returns of 22% every year. At its peak, the biggest fund that Galleon owned was estimated at nearly $7 billion.

Investigators soon found that those returns were garnered through insider trading. Rajaratnam used his social network with people like the owner of the McKinsey & Company, Rajat Gupta, to secure insider data about their dealings and tech stocks. Before the news became public, Rajaratnam would buy or sell his stocks based on this data.

Overall, the hedge funds began to grow in value to over $60 million, which became the biggest insider trading case in US history. He also conspired to get confidential information of Goldman preferred stock before the $5 billion purchase of Berkshire Hathaway by Warren Buffett. His friend, Rajat Gupta, gave him all the details since he would also profit from the stock purchase agreement as the would-be chairman of Galleon.

Raj Rajaratnam was found guilty on 14 counts of security fraud and sentenced to 11 years in prison. He also has to pay a civil and criminal penalty of over $150 million. This was the longest prison sentence to have been handed out for a crime like insider trading, but it was also the biggest hedge fund crime according to the Justice Department. Gupta was also charged in 2011 by the SEC in an administrative proceeding. Gupta pleaded not guilty and counter-sued. He won the administrative charge but was later arrested following criminal charges.

Hiromasa Ezoe

Hiromasa Ezoe became famous when the Recruit Scandal broke out in Tokyo, Japan.

The scandal involved many prominent Japanese politicians who were part of insider trading and corruption conspiracy. The scandal actually led to most of them sending in their resignations in 1988.

Recruit was a classified and human resources company which worked in Tokyo. Hiromasa Ezoe was the chairman of the firm who offered a number of shares of a subsidiary, Cosmos, to senior politicians and leaders in Japan. This was before Cosmos went public in 1986 and its share price sky-rocketed. The politicians who had invested in the company each saw a profit return of ¥66 million on average. There were 17 members of Diet that were involved in insider trading but an additional 30 also took 'special favors' from Recruit to further their gains. Huge politicians like Prime Minister

Noboru Takeshita, Chief Cabinet Secretary Takao Fujinami, and former Prime Minister Yasuhiro Nakasone were all embroiled in the scandal. Other leaders of political parties like the Democratic Party of Japan, Komeito, Japan Socialist Party, as well as employees of the LDP government were all involved in this corruption. Chairmen of popular companies like Nihon Keizai Shimbun, Yomiuri Shimbun, and NTT also used the information to boost their own profits.

The Recruit scandal was so vast that it ended up crossing party lines. Hiromasa Ezoe resorted to insider trading to reach the pockets of every major politician in the country including those in power under the LDP government. He would have been able to yield a lot of political power with the briberies he had made.

Ezoe was arrested in 1989 but the trial went on for 13 years since it was such a vast operation. After over 300 court appearance, in 2003, he was finally sentenced to 3 years in prison which was later suspended. He ended up serving no actual time for the Recruit Scandal and he passed away in 2013. The Japanese political system is actually really expensive and politicians commonly invest in businesses to fund their campaigns.

In turn, businesses also need political support to expand in the country. This is the reason why it is so common to corruption and bribery in Japan. In America, such close ties among politicians and businesses are discouraged often and would never be allowed by the general public and law.

Andrew Fastow

Andrew Stuart Fastow was born in 1961 and was a businessman and the Chief Financial Officer at Enron Corporation. Enron was an energy trading company in Houston, Texas. He was fired from the firm shortly before the company went bankrupt. Andrew Fastow was the mind behind their vast off-balance sheets that hid the company's massive losses. He made special purpose entities based on the limited partnerships that Enron controlled to hide the fact that the company wasn't making any money.

The US energy market went through a long period of deregulation in the 1990s which provided Enron with huge trading opportunities. They were able to buy energy from cheaper producers and sell it in other markets at floating prices. Fastow was a mastermind at manipulating the markets in order to make Enron more cash. Jeffrey Skilling, the chief executive officer of Enron, saw the skill Fastow had and worked closely with him. They, along with Enron founder Kenneth Lay, came up with new ways to keep the stock price of the company up even though it wasn't truly making any profits.

Fastow began to design an intricate web of companies that only did business with Enron. These ghost companies allowed the company to show profits it didn't have and raised money for the company for future ventures. The debt section of the balance sheet was clean even though in reality the company was in 30 billion dollars of debt. He also neglected basic financial practices like cash on hand and other total liabilities. He used threats of losing all future business to pressure some of the biggest banks in the country like Citibank and Merril Lynch to invest in his funds. When these banks' and firms' analysts reported the negative ratings of Enron to discourage these investments, he had them fired.

He illegally maintained personal stakes in these independent ghost entities that hid the true nature of profits by Enron. He did this directly or even through partners like Michael Kopper. This resulted in him defrauding the company out of tens of millions of dollars. The U.S. Securities and Exchange Commission has to open an investigation into the company conduct and Fastow's role in fraudulent behavior in 2001. Kopper also pleaded guilty to the scam Fastow had launched. His wife also worked at Enron alongside him. Lea Weingarten was an assistant treasurer who committed money laundering, wire fraud, and filed fraudulent income tax returns.

He was actually so good at hiding the losses of the company that a year before Enron was forced to declare bankruptcy and was near financial collapse, the stock price of Enron was at an all-time high of $90. Enron told its employees to invest their retirement savings in Enron stock right before it dropped to 40 cents per share when it declared it was broke. Fastow was charged and had to serve a prison sentence of 6 years. His wife served jail time as well before she was released to a halfway house.

Dennis Kozlowski

Leo Dennis Kozlowski was born in 1946 was the former CEO of Tyco International. Under his leadership, Tyco continued to expand during the 1990s. The company continued to beat Wall Street expectation and became bigger with strategic acquisitions and mergers. It became a mega-conglomerate. Kozlowski finally left Tyco in 2002 over a controversy with his compensation package.

He was convicted in 2005 for giving unauthorized bonuses to himself worth $81 million and used Tyco funds to purchase art worth $14.7 million. He also used the company funds to give $20 million as banking fee to Frank Walsh who was a former Tyco director. He was tried twice since the first trial was ruled as a mistrial. One of the jurors made an OK sign to Kozlowski's lawyers and was then threatened by the public. In the second trial, Kozlowski testified on his own behalf. He stated that he had never committed a crime while he was the CEO but that his pay package may have been 'almost embarrassingly 'big' or 'confusing'.

Kozlowski was known for his extravagant lifestyle that was supported by the booming stock market. He made Tyco pay for his luxurious $30 million New York City apartment, complete with $15,000 "dog umbrella stands" and $6,000 shower curtains. Forbes also reported that he purchased several acres in The Sanctuary in Boca Raton which is a private gated community. He had huge parties like the $2 million party for his wife's birthday on the Italian island of Sardinia. Half of the bill for the party was paid by Tyco since he insisted that the party would be the perfect location to court shareholders. He even had an oceanfront estate on the Nantucket Island worth millions of dollars.

He was sentenced to a minimum of 8 years and 4 months in prison and an aggregate maximum of 25 years. He was denied parole in 2012 but was granted a conditional release in 2014 from the Lincoln Correctional Facility. He and his partner in crime Swartz were ordered by the court to pay a total fine of $134 million in restitution. Swartz was fined an additional $35 million, and Kozlowski was also fined $70 million. Together they were charged and convicted on 22 counts of falsifying business records, securities fraud conspiracy, and grand larceny.

Anthony Elgindy

Anthony Elgindy was born in 1967 and was the founder of Pacific Equity Investigations. He was a car salesman in San Diego and became a stock trader in 1988. He moved to Armstrong McKinley soon, turned into an informer and helped get the firm shut down for taking bribes to recommend the stock. He went viral in 1995 when he became a short seller. He became known for exposing companies that he thought were conducting some illegal or unethical activity to inflate their stock prices.

Elgindy became so famous for his comments and analysis on short-selling message boards that he was able to send stock on a downward spiral with just one post. He soon launched Pacific Equity Investigations based on his earlier experience at exposing fraud in the boiler rooms.

During the 2000s, Elgindy partnered with an FBI agent called Jeff Broyer. He gave Broyer names of the firms that he believed were engaging in illegal activities. Broyer began to use FBI databases to find information on any investigations by the SEC or FBI of the companies in question. The agent funneled information of the investigations to Elgindy who used the information to tank the stock of the firms. He began to extort the executives of the companies in question into giving him the stock of their company if they wanted his attacks to stop.

The National Association of Securities Dealers (NASD) ruled in 2003 that Elgindy and his firm engaged in manipulative schemes in 1997. These schemes led to the artificial inflation of the share prices of Saf T Lok, Inc. since fraudulent quotations were entered into the NASDAQ's system. He was also shorting the stock at artificially high prices and then made negative research comments to depress the share price of Saf T Lok. Key West Securities and Elgindy had their NASD license revoked and was fined $51,000. A year later the ban was lifted by the SEC on appeal.

Before the ban was lifted, an investigation had already been launched on Elgindy by the FBI. This was from a tip that showed he had locked in his profits the day of the 9/11 attacks, implying that he knew about the attacks beforehand. They weren't able to find any evidence on the tip, but they did uncover his scheme to steal confidential information using the FBI for his own profits. They questioned their FBI employee, Broyer, who resigned rather than face an inquiry. Broyer began to work directly with Elgindy, and his girlfriend, Lynn Wingate, who worked for the FBI and continued to funnel information to Elgindy. In 2002, all three of them were indicted for their roles in the schemes to make money from confidential information.

In 2005, Elgindy was charged with securities fraud, racketeering and a host of other crimes connected to stealing confidential information about different firms from the SEC and FBI. He was also accused of using insider trading on 32 different stocks including Genesis Intermedia, Inc. He was convicted on five of those insider trading stocks for his illegal gain of $66,000. He was sentenced to 11 years in prison and was released in 2013. In 2015, he committed suicide.

Tang Wanxin

Tang Wanxin was just a simple tomato farmer in China with his brother. They managed to turn their simple tomato farm into one of the largest companies in China. His company, D'Long International, owned and invested in several financial services and industrial operations including construction materials, food, machinery, and financial sectors.

In order to allow his company to expand, Tang was in need of some serious investment money. He ended up using illicit means to gather the funds for his company. Beijing filed charges against managers at

D'Long and Tang for using illegal means to raise $5.6 billion from the public in 2001 and 2004. He was one of the richest men in China when he was charged with personal assets estimated at 2 billion yuan ($300 million). The charges implicated more than 32,000 individuals and 2,500 organizations.

A swift trial later, Tang was found guilty for manipulating stock prices and illegally raising capital for his company's expansion. Although he was one of the richest tycoons in China, his personal assets were seized by the government and he was sentenced to 8 years in prisons.

Bernard Ebbers

Bernard John "Bernie" Ebbers was born in 1941 and was a Canadian businessman. He founded a company called WorldCom as a

Chief Executive Officer. It was the second largest accounting scandal after the Madoff schemes in the history of the United States.

Ebbers started his business career while operating a chain of motels in Mississippi and joined many others as an investor for the Long Distance Discount Services, Inc. (LDDS) in 1993. After two years he was appointed as the chief executive of the firm. The company soon began to expand by acquiring over 60 other independent telecommunications firms.

It changed its name to WorldCom in 1995 and a year later acquired MFS Communications, Inc., taking in UUNet as well. This was one of the largest acquisitions in US history at $12 billion but was later dwarfed by larger deals like WorldCom's proposed acquisition of MCI at $40 billion. Bernard Ebbers received a public notice in 1997 after he had announced that he was making an unsolicited bid for one of the biggest communication company called MCI. He still managed to successfully acquire MCI in 1998, despite the public notice and any other barriers that followed.

He proceeded to receive multiple accolades from the press like Member of Wired 25, Mississippi Business Hall of Fame, Time Digital 50, and many others. In 1990, he announced that the next company he would acquire would be MCI WorldCom's biggest rival called Sprint Communications. However, this idea was later abandoned after antitrust regulators began to raise objections on his growing monopoly. The protests, combined with the general downturn of the telecom industry, led to a fall in WorldCom's stock price.

Ebber's many personal holdings were actually purchased with loans that he had backed by the stock holdings of WorldCom. His personal holdings included a 500,000 acre Douglas Lake Canada's biggest ranch, a 21,000 acres Angelina Plantation, 540,000 acres of Joshua Holdings, Pine Ridge Farm, Columbus Lumber, a Trucking firm, several yachts, nine hotels, and investments in a minor league hockey team. When the stock price declined after protests, he began to receive several calls to provide additional collateral for his loans. To prevent Ebber from selling his share to return pay off his loans, WorldCom directors authorized many loan guarantees and loans for him. When he resigned in 2002, his loans were consolidated into one $408.2 million promissory note.

Two months after his resignation from WorldCom in 2002, the company admitted to $3.9 billion in accounting misstatements. This number eventually grew to $11 billion, and it launched multiple investigations, most of which focused around Ebber.

In 2003, an attorney filed 15 counts against Ebbers for violation of state's securities law. The charge sheet claimed that he had defrauded investors on many occasions so that they would invest more money into the firm. Ebber was found guilty in 2005 for nine felony charges include false statements to securities regulators and conspiracy and securities fraud. He was sentenced to 25 years in prison and is set for release in 2028 when he will be 86 years old.

John J. Rigas

John James Rigas was born in 1924 and founded the largest cable TV company in America called Adelphia Communications Corporation. The Rigas cable television firm started in Coudersport where the Rigas family purchased the town's cable franchise. John and his brother, Gus, bought out the partners in an effort to grow the company. To do this, they borrowed large sums of money to buy out other cable companies, in turn, creating a regional monopoly. This meant that Adelphia became the largest cable provider in South Florida, Pittsburgh, Cleveland, and Philadelphia. The company had over 5.6 million customers and reached over 30 states in America. It began to expand its services and launched products like long-distance telephone services and high-speed cable Internet services.

He also owned the Buffalo Sabres, a National Hockey League, where he installed his son, Timothy, as president. He even re-launched the Wellsville Nitros as a college summer baseball team. With his newfound money, he contributed $50,750 to the Republican Party since he respected Republican family values and their core free-market policies. Like many Wall Street members, he attempted to gain political sway through his donations to the political party.

In 2002, he resigned from his position of CEO at Adelphia Communications Corporation. This resignation was sent in after he was indicted for wire fraud, securities fraud, and bank fraud. His sons and two other executives of the company were also charged since they also participated in these crimes as well. They were accused of stealing from the company by hiding $2.3 billion in liabilities from investors who were pooling their resources into the company. They also routinely used corporation funds for their own personal expenses and investments.

In 2004, Rigas was convicted of these charges and a year later was sentenced to 15 years in prison. When the firm had to acknowledge the $3.1 billion in loans that the Rigas family didn't record in the books, it was forced to file for bankruptcy. In 2005, Timothy Rigas pleaded not guilty to charges of tax evasion. In 2012, this charge was officially dismissed, and he was set free. However, John's arrest meant that the NHL stripped him of his presidency over the Sabres, a NHL team.

In 2015, Rigas appealed for compassionate release due to his diagnosis of bladder cancer. He was released in 2016.

Samuel D. Waksal

Samuel D. "Sam" Waksal was born in 1947 and founded the biopharmaceutical company called ImClone Systems in 1984. He also founded Kadmon Pharmaceuticals, which he financed with commended operations in New York City and private capital.

ImClone Systems was involved in different development projects and research before it filed for its first Biologic License Application in 2001. Waksal led the development of a drug for cancer patients called Erbitux. After winning the rights for the cancer antibody and general clinical success, the stock for ImClone skyrocketed to over $70 a share. Due to the popularity of the drug, Bristol-Myers Squibb even signed $2 billion for marketing rights for Erbitux in 2001. However, the same year the FDA issued a Refusal to File due to some concerns it had over the structure of the clinical trials. While the drug was under further review with the Food and Drug Administration (FDA), Waskal became involved in a scandal for insider trading.

Even with the looming scandal, the drug still got approved by the FDA in 2004. The drug was able to generate $1.5 billion in sales in 2008 and was credited with helping thousands of cancer patients. ImClone was bought by Eli Lilly and Company for the steep price of $6.5 billion the very same year due to the rising scandals with Waksal.

Waksal became aware of the FDA's 2001 rejection on Christmas and couldn't get FDA to reconsider. They began to draft a press release to announce the rejection by the FDA when businesses close on December 28. Until the announcement, Waksal was banned from telling anyone about the pending rejection or selling the stock of his company. However, he was aware of the number of financial problems that would come about after the public release of Erbitux. One of the problems that hounded Waksal was that he had already executed a warrant to buy ImClone shares as collateral in exchange for a loan from the Bank of America in 2000 before pledging another one. When it would be discovered that the

2000 warrant was no longer valid, Waksal would definitely be charged with bank fraud. So, he tipped off his family and friends to sell their ImClone stock before the public release. Peter Bacanovic, Waksal's broker, also alerted his mutual friend, Martha Stewart, that ImClone was about to lose stock value.

Waksal was arrested in 2002 for insider trading and 4 months later pleaded guilty to charges of bank fraud, obstruction of justice, perjury, and securities fraud. In 2003, he also pled guilty to wire fraud and conspiracy to avoid $1.2 million in sales taxes for different artworks that were worth $15 million.

Samuel Waksal was sentenced to 7 years and 3 months in federal prison and had to pay $4 million in back taxes and fines. This sentence was the maximum punishment allowed under law, and he went to the Federal Correctional Institution in Schuylkill. He was released in 2009 after serving his time.

Joseph Nacchio

Joseph P. Nacchio was born in 1949 and served as the Chief Executive Officer and chairman at Qwest Communications International. He left AT&T Corporation to join Qwest in 1997. While he was working with Qwest as chairman, he was serving on two federal advisory panels. Due to this, he was given top secret security clearance for the National Security Telecommunications Advisory Committee in the 1990s.

In 2000, Qwest acquired the regional rival called US West and became one of the largest communications company in the region. Two years later, the company was forced to admit to false accounting during the merger. While it was under investigation, Nacchio was the only head at the communications company who demanded approval under the Foreign Intelligence Surveillance Act or a court order to turn over the communication records to NSA. He began to claim that the NSA was punishing Qwest by dropping a million dollar contract after Qwest refused to participate in a surveillance program. While this investigation was happening, the company's stock began to decline from $38 to $2. Due to this, Nacchio resigned in 2002 and was replaced by Richard Notebaert, the former CEO of Ameritech.

In 2005, Nacchio and 6 other former executives of Qwest were sued by the U.S.

Securities and Exchange Commission for financial fraud. They were accused of benefiting from the artificially inflated stock price and taking part in a $3 billion financial fraud scheme. The government accused Nacchio of fraud since he continued to tell Wall Street that Qwest would be able to achieve its targets of aggressive revenue even after he knew it would be impossible. This lie was what helped the company acquire US West. In Nacchio's defense, he had thought that Qwest would be receiving some large government contracts soon. However, he did sell his own shares before the imminent announcement of the government contracts. He claimed he had done so because he wasn't in the right state of mind due to problems with his son.

Despite all these claims, Nacchio was indicted in 2005 for insider trading charges and had to surrender his passport since he was considered as a flight risk. He was charged with 42 counts of insider trading with each count leading to a potential 10-year sentence. He was convicted of 19 counts of insider trading in 2007 to six years in prison, had to pay $19 million in fines, and was forced to forfeit the $52 million he had gained in illegal stock sales. His sentence ended in 2013.

Allen Stanford

Robert Allen Stanford was born in 1950 and was a former American financer and even sponsored many professional sports teams. He was the chairman at Stanford Financial Group of Companies and contributed millions of dollars to politicians in the United States and Antigua –of which he had dual citizenship.

In 2009, an investigation was launched into the Stanford Financial Group by the FBI, SEC, Financial Industry Regulatory Authority, and the Florida Office of Financial Regulation. This investigation was launched due to the consistent higher-than-market profits Stanford International Bank continued to claim to its potential depositors. A former executive turned into an informant and told SEC officials how Stanford continually presented hypothetical investment results as historical data to the clients and investors during sales pitches.

Stanford was accused of claiming that his deposit certificates were safe as -or even safer than- that of the insured accounts by US governments. In 2006, the US Embassy in the Bahamas reported to the investigators that Stanford's companies often engaged in bribery, political manipulation, and money laundering.

In 2009, several federal agents raided the Stanford Financial offices and treated it similar to a crime scene. Stanford was charged with massive fraud that revolved around the $8 billion investment scheme of the firm. His personal and company assets were all frozen and placed under a US federal judge. Stanford was also forced to surrender his passport since he was deemed a flight risk after he was reported as attempting to flee the country on the day of the raids.

Stanford was arrested in 2009 for falsifying records to hide fraud, misappropriating investors' money, and operating a massive Ponzi scheme. He pled not guilty to the charges and went through a series of scams to get out of his sentencing. He was admitted to Regional Medical Center for claims of a racing heart while he was being taken from prison to his first hearing. A month later, he was hospitalized again after being 'severely' beaten by another inmate; his plea to change to a more secure facility was rejected after the injuries were described as 'non-life threatening'. SEC Inspector General H. David

Kotz who was investigating the case was also removed for a 'conflict of interest'. Stanford also claimed that he would not be able to take the stand in 2011 due to amnesia from the injuries he had sustained from his fight with the inmate. He was reported competent enough to stand trial.

Despite these attempts, in 2012, he was sentenced to 110 years in federal prison and had to forfeit $5.9 billion. His earliest possible release is in 2105 when he will be 155 years old.

Stanford was also investigated for Tax Liens when the court found him and his wife had under-reported almost half a million in their 1990 federal taxes. From 2007-2008, Stanford had four federal tax liens against him totaling more than $212 million. He is also under investigation for money laundering for a Mexican Gulf cartel. He also had a trust for his mistress and two children in the Swiss and Isle of Man bank accounts worth $2.5 million. Stanford was also involved in Trademark infringement after his claim that his relative founded Stanford University.

Conclusion

Wall Street has a reputation for producing a huge crop of people who think they are above the law. They have been responsible for swindling thousands of people out of their hard-earned cash and using their profits to manipulate politics and the national economy. It was the actions of such chairmen and owners that led to the closing of many firms, robbing hundreds of their careers.

Wall Street has been using the power and sway of such people to further their own gains for a long time now. However, it is also important to note that regulations by the government and public pressure have been keeping Wall Street greed under control. These notorious Wall Street criminals had luxurious lives and spent millions on their own desires. Nevertheless, at the end of the day, they had to pay the price since they were all prosecuted by the law. These wolfs of wall street were all eventually placed on a leash, stopping them from wrecking havoc to the economy.